I want to dedicate this book to:
my husband Michael
for all of his creativity & hard work;
my daughters
Molly, Khloe & Roxie-Jane;
and my grandchildren
Charlee, Jude & Cash.

From our readers:

Sin-D's journey serves as an important lesson in understanding how to build self-worth through faith and kindness. The story highlights the struggles of bullying in a relatable, age-appropriate way, allowing children to see the impact of their words and actions on others. Through Sin-D's experiences, children are taught the value of self-love and the importance of seeing themselves as God's creation, uniquely special and loved. This book is perfect for both parents and teachers looking to address issues like bullying, self-esteem, and kindness with young readers. Its Christian perspective adds a valuable dimension to the conversation about self-worth, making it a great resource for faith-based education or just a meaningful story to read at home. *-Whitney Hill*

Your book was so funny, cute, and creative! It's a wonderful way to teach children about Jesus and his love for us! *-Rayne Johnson*

I love Karolrae's Book. It is very interesting and informative. I love the illustrations. *-Glenda Southerland*

This is a well-written and beautifully illustrated piece of children's literature. The main character's involvement in a variety of comical shenanigans is relatable to a broad based audience. I am excited about sharing this captivating character building series with my first grade students! *-Angie Lang*

The Sin-D the Scientist book was a great read, and I loved the books' faith-based message about self-esteem for children. My daughter and I enjoyed the vibrant illustrations and exciting characters, especially Sin-D and her wacky experiments. This book is a wonderful addition to any child's library. *-Rachael Willingham*

Hi! My name is Sin-D the Scientist.

I LOVE CHEMISTRY AND ENJOY DOING EXPERIMENTS,

I ONCE MIXED THE WRONG CHEMICALS WITH NITROGEN AND THEY BLEW UP IN MY FACE!

SOME CALL ME "SINNER SIN-D" BECAUSE THE FIRST THREE LETTERS OF MY NAME ARE S-I-N. THEY SPELL "SIN".

THEY MAKE ME FEEL SPECIAL LIKE A SUPER HERO!

PAGE 6

IT HAS A TENDENCY TO GIVE ME A NEW LOOK.

PAGE 9

HE WANTS YOU TO FOCUS ON THE NEGATIVE.

HE DOESN'T WANT YOU TO DO WHAT IS GOOD, TRUE & RIGHT!

PAGE 16

WE HAVE SO MANY EMOTIONS THAT WE FACE AND WE'VE GOT TO UNDERSTAND AND LEARN HOW TO DEAL WITH THEM PROPERLY.

When I get made fun of, sometimes I laugh along. Sometimes I cry.

Can you relate?

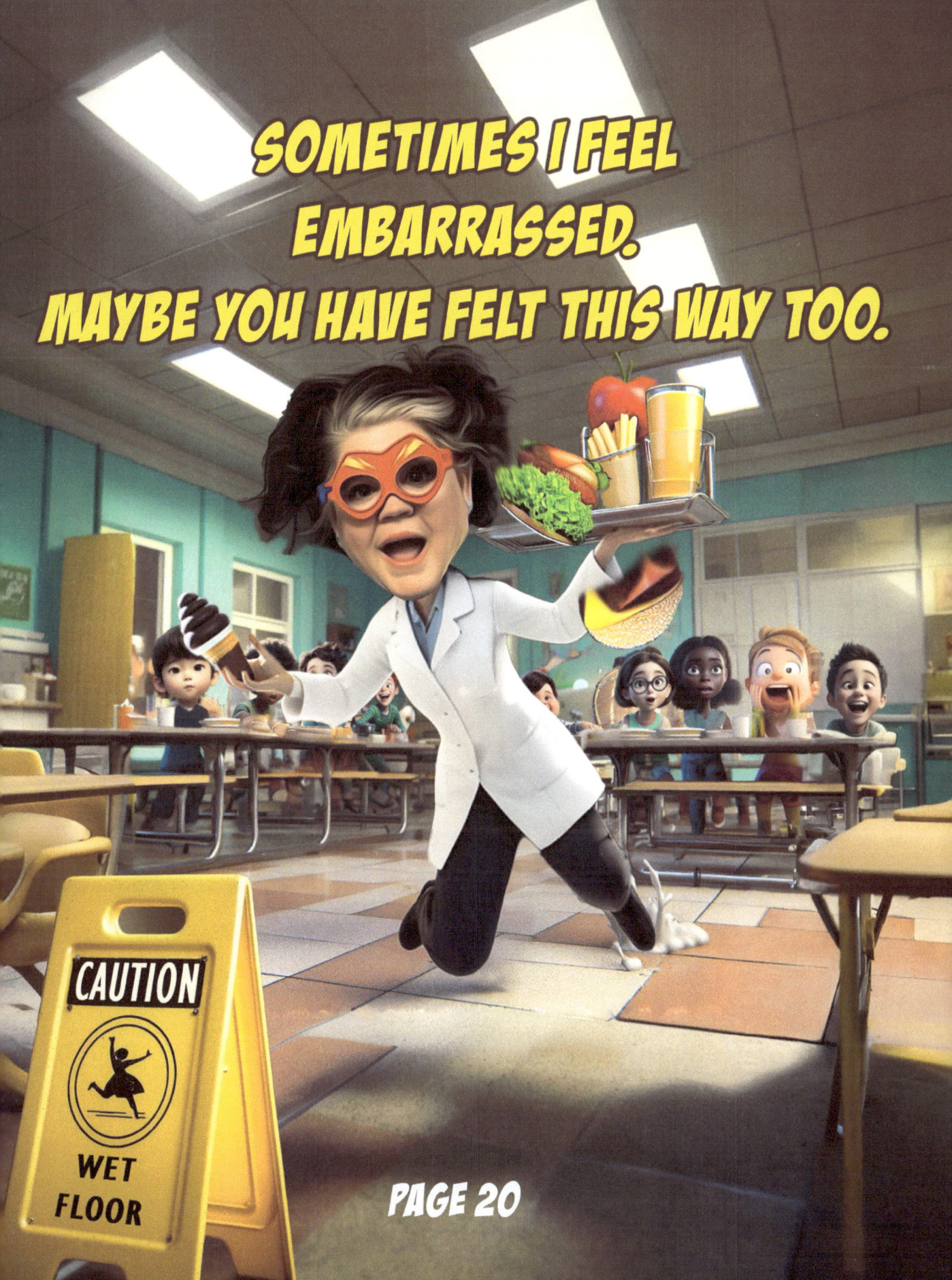

SOMETIMES I STAND UP FOR MYSELF AND LET THOSE BULLIES KNOW THAT THEY ARE HURTING MY FEELINGS AND THAT MAKES JESUS SAD.

PAGE 21

A GREAT WAY TO DEAL WITH YOUR HEARTACHES AND BULLIES IS TO PRAY FOR THEM.

JESUS SAYS IN THE SCRIPTURE TO PRAY FOR YOUR ENEMIES.

43 "You have heard that it was said, 'You shall love your neighbor and hate your enemy.' 44 But I say to you, love your enemies, bless those who curse you, do good to those who hate you, and pray for those who spitefully use you and persecute you,
Matthew 5:43,44

I KNOW IT'S NOT ALWAYS EASY TO PRAY AND FORGIVE.

PAGE 24

But did you know that Jesus says we are to forgive 70 x 7?

PAGE 25

...WEAR THE CROWN THAT YOUR HEAVENLY FATHER INTENDED FOR YOU TO WEAR.

www.ingramcontent.com/pod-product-compliance
Lightning Source LLC
LaVergne TN
LVHW070434070526
838199LV00014B/503